Little Machines

*28 Short Mechanical Works
for Unaccompanied Mixed Voices*

by Secretary Michael

LITTLE MACHINES (28 Short Mechanical Works for Unaccompanied Mixed Voices)
Composer: Secretary Michael

ISBN: 978-1-888712-42-1

TYPEFACES USED:
Body: Adobe Garamond Pro
Headings: Monotype Corsiva

Machinists Union Press
St. Louis, Missouri

Contents

1. B-flat is the Answer

(from "Little Machines")

Secretary Michael
Johannes Brahms, 1868

♩=66   B♭

Open-Minded Sopranos

C D B___ C D B C D B_

Wise Altos

Open-Minded Tenors

A___ C E A

Close-Minded Basses

B - flat is the an-swer.   B - flat is the an - swer.   B - flat is the

6   F⁷

_ C D B_ C D B_ C D B_ C D B_ C D B_

There are those who seem strange and who ne - ver much change. Have the

C_ E A C_ E A C_ E A C_ E A C_ E A

an - swer.   B - flat is the an - swer.   B - flat is the an - swer.

11
B♭
— C D B— C D B— C D B— C D B—
an - swer, so they claim, and it's al ways the same. Let them
— C— E A— C— E A— C— E A— C— E A—
B - flat is the an - swer. B - flat is the an - swer.
15
E♭ B♭ E♭ B♭
— C D B— C D B— C D B— C D B—
live, let them grow, let them sing what they know. For it
— C— E A— C— E A— C— E A— C— E A—
B - flat is the an - swer. B - flat is the an - swer.
19
E♭ B♭ Cm F B♭
— C D B— C D B— B- flat.—
may just be that: that the an swer is B - flat.—
— C— E A— C— B— B - flat.—
B - flat is the an - swer. B - flat is the an - swer.

2. Chance to Start Again

(from "Little Machines")

Secretary Michael
Roud #6294

♩=76

Bass Ostin.

D / A / A⁷ / D / D⁷ / G

May e - v'ry night end with light and a brand new day be - gin. May

e - v'ry wrong end with right and a chance to start a -

G / D / A / A⁷ / D / D⁷ / G

Cntr Mel

May e - v'ry night end with light and a brand new day be - gin. May

Bass Ostin.

gain. May e - v'ry night end with light and a brand new day be - gin. May

D / A / F# / G / A⁷ / D / D

e - v'ry wrong end with right and a chance to start a - gain. A chance to start a -

e - v'ry wrong end with right and a chance to start a - gain. A chance to start a -

A / A⁷ / D / D⁷ / G / D / A / F#

gain for all a chance to start a - gain. May e - v'ry night end with light and a

gain for all a chance to start a - gain. May e - v'ry night end with light and a

Mel (m. 20):
May e - v'ry night end with light and a brand new day be-gin. May e - v'ry wrong end with right and a chance to start a - gain. A chance to start a - gain for all a chance to start a - gain. May e - v'ry night end with light and a chance to start a - gain. May gain.

Cntr Mel:
chance to start a - gain. May e - v'ry night end with light and a brand new day be-gin. May e - v'ry wrong end with right and a chance to start a - gain. A chance to start a - gain for all a chance to start a - gain. May e - v'ry night end with light and a chance to start a - gain. May gain.

Bass Ostin.:
chance to start a - gain. May e - v'ry night end with light and a brand new day be-gin. May e - v'ry wrong end with right and a chance to start a - gain. A chance to start a - gain for all a chance to start a - gain. May e - v'ry night end with light and a chance to start a - gain. May gain.

3. Dreams

(from "Little Machines")

Secretary Michael
Stephen Foster, 1862

♩.=48

Dreamers *(Counter-Melody)*

C

Dreams, Dreams, just dream-ing of

Snores *(Men)*

INHALED SNORES: *(bass clef) are snorted, unvocalized yet pitched (from mouth shape).*
EXHALED SNORES: *(treble clef) are either whistled or created with an unvocalized yet pitched "sh" sound.*

5   Dm   G⁷   C

Dreams,   Dreams,   just dream-ing   of   Dreams,   Dreams,   just dream-ing   of   Dreams._____

8   C   Dm   G⁷

Melody

Se - cret dreams,   they   wi ther and die.   Life takes o ver, not   tel - ling us

Dreamers *(Counter-Melody)*

Dreams,   Dreams, just dream-ing of Dreams,   Dreams, just dream ing of Dreams,   Dreams, just dream ing of

Snores *(Men)*

why.____ Shar - ing our dreams is what we must do.

Dreams.____ Dreams, Dreams, just dream-ing of Dreams, Dreams, just dream ing of

Dreams dreamt to - ge - ther are dreams that come true. true.

Dreams, Dreams, just dream - ing of Dreams.____ Dreams.

(Snoring stops)

Melody
Dream of the fu - ture, not of the past.____ Dreams shared with o - thers are

Dreamers (Counter-Melody)
Dream of the fu - ture, not of the past. Dreams shared with o - thers are

Tenor Bass
Dream____ Dream____ Dream____

10

Notes

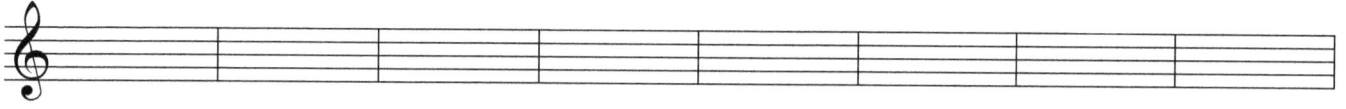

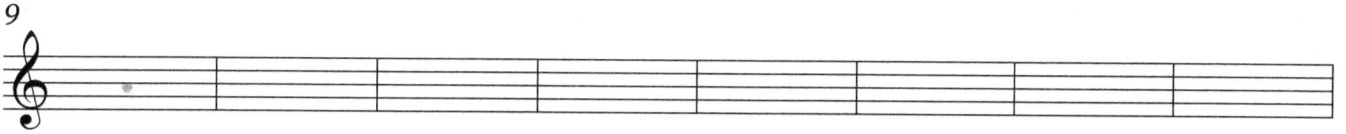

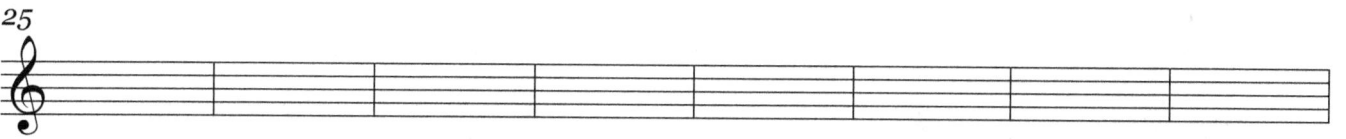

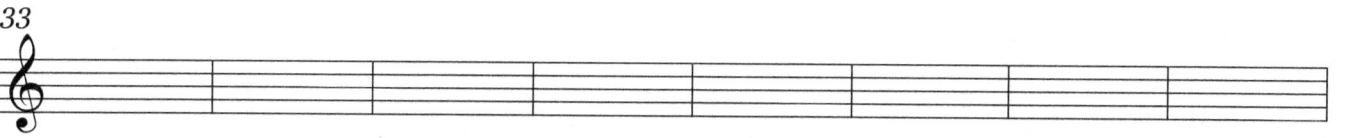

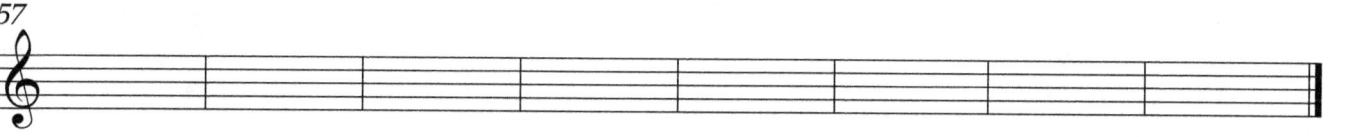

4. Education for All

(from "Little Machines")

Secretary Michael
Edward Elgar, 1901

♩=76

Middle Voices: For the big and for the small, e - du - ca - tion is for all.

Middle Voices: For the big and for the small, e - du - ca - tion is for all.

Lower Voices: For big, for small,_ e - du - ca - ca is for all.___

Upper (Mel.): For those who are rich,_____ for those who are poor._____

Middle: For_ those are rich are rich, for_ those are poor are poor.

Lower: For those rich, rich,_ for those poor, poor._

[Upper]: For those we ad - mire,_____ for those we ig - nore._____

[Middle]: For those ad - mire, ad - mire, for those we ig - nore.

[Lower]: For_ those ad - mire, ad - mire,_ for_ those we nore, ig - nore.

33
C G7 Am C F C D7 G7
For those who climb, for those who fall.
For those who climb who climb, for those who fall who fall.
For those climb, climb, for those fall, fall.
41
C D7 Gmaj7 Em7 Dm G7 C Cmaj7 C7
For old and young, for big and small.
For old and young and young, for big and small.
For old and young and young, for big and small and small.
49
F G7 Cmaj7 Am Dm7 G7 C
This, this is our bond: E - du - ca-tion for all!
This, this, this is our bond our bond: E - du - ca-tion for all!
This this bond bond: E - du - ca-tion for all!

The different melodies are to be added cumulatively (see instructions).
Singers can more easily sing from the individual country scores than from this full score.

5. Everywhere the Beautiful

(from "Little Machines")

Secretary Michael

♩=76

Mel.1 Russia: Rus - sia, a - bun - dant Rus - sia, full of

Mel.2 Kenya: Li - ons and cro - co - diles, e - ven the wart - hog smiles.

Mel.3 China: The beau - ty of Chi - na, it

Mel.4 Cuba: The beau - ty is a - live in Cu - ba,___ from co - ral reef to moun - tain top,___ from

Mel.5 Amer.: Oh beau - ti - ful for spa - cious skies, for

3

1. na - ture, full of rich - es, full of his - - to - ry. From the Gol - den

2. Ze - bras, gi - raffes, all here in Ken - ya, the beau - ty of A - fri - ca.

3. grows a - cross the cen - - tu - ries. From

4. dark - est cave to spar - k'ling wet - lands___ our beau - ty ne - ver ne - ver stops. The

5. am - ber waves of grain. For

Measure 5:

1. Moun - tains, to the U - ral trea - - sures, to the

2. Pe - li - cans spread their wings, os - tri - ches try to sing fla -

3. fer - - tile Yel - low Ri - - ver plain, the

4. fish and wild-life thrive in Cu - ba, _____ from hum-ming-birds to paint-ed snails, from

5. pur - - ple moun - tains ma - - je - sty a -

Measure 7:

1. Cau - cu - sus be - tween the seas. _____ From the Ko -mi

2. min-goes and cranes and par-rots with brains, we're all kinds of fea-thers sing-ing to-ge-ther.

3. com - mon strug - gle still sus - tains the

4. ti - ny bats to crabs and tur - tles, _____ from cro-co-diles to sharks and whales. The

5. bove the frui - ted plain. A -

9 [C] ... [G]

1. Fo - rests, to the Arc - tic tun - dra, to the
2. And un-der-neath the spar-kl-ing wa - ter__ the mar-lins and dol-phins play
3. beau - - ty of Chi - - na from
4. beau-ty is a-live in Cu - ba,_____ pro-tec-ted by di-ver-si-ty,__ an
5. mer - - i - ca, A - mer - - i - ca, for -

11 [G⁷] ... [C] ... [C⁷]

1. won -ders of Kam-chat-ka in the East. May we
2. Tu na fish hur - tles_ past ur-chins and tur - tles,_ past oc-to-pus and Man-ta ray._ And
3. Yun - nan jun - gle to the Go - - bi sands. May
4. is land that is clean and heal - thy,_____ the way the earth would want to be._ The
5. e - ver may we be a

13

F   C

1. share them, and like the Vol - ga may we

2. who is the ste - ward who keeps this in bal - ance, pro - tec-ting our di - ver - si - ty?

3. Yang - tze's course re - main a source of

4. beau-ty is a-live in Cu - ba, we live it e - v'ry sin - gle day. En -

5. place where there is beau - ty from

15

Dm⁷   G⁷   C

1. flow in beau - ty and peace.

2. Ken-ya the beau - ty, Ken-ya the beau - ty, the keep-er of our de - sti - ny.

3. peace and beau - ty to all of Man.

4. vi - ro-men-tal re - vo - lu - tion! And Cu - ba we will lead the way!

5. sea to shi - ning sea.

*When sung as the 1st melody in "Everywhere the Beautiful", "Russia the Beautiful"
should be sung once strongly, then repeated softly during all the melodies that follow
(to create a supportive harmonic foundation).*

5. Russia the Beautiful (Melody 1)

(from "Little Machines")

Secretary Michael

♩ = 76

Rus - sia, a - bun-dant Rus - sia, full of na-ture, full of rich-es, full of his - to - ry. From the Gol-den Moun-tains, to the U - ral trea - sures, to the Cau - cu - sus be-tween the seas. From the Ko - mi Fo - rests, to the Arc - tic tun - dra, to the won-ders of Kam-chat - ka in the East. May we share them, and like the Vol - ga may we flow in beau-ty___ and peace.

Golden Mountains: "Golden Mountains of Altai" is an important region in Siberia distinguished
by its biodiversity and chosen as a UNESCO World Heritage Site;
Urals: refers to the Ural Mountains, the mountain range that runs north-south through Russia,
dividing Europe from Asia. These mountains are rich in ores and minerals.
Caucusus: refers to the Caucusus Mountains, a biodiverse range that runs east-west between the
Black and Caspian Seas; contains Europe's highest peak (Mt. Elbrus) and divides Europe from Asia.
Komi Forests: largest virgin forest in Europe, located in the northern Ural Mountains;
Chosen as a UNESCO World Heritage Site;
Kamchatka: refers to the beautiful volcanic Kamchatka Peninsula in the Russian Far East;
known as the "land of fire and ice", the biodiverse area contains a UNESCO World Heritage Site;
Volga: refers to the Volga River, the longest river in Europe;

When sung as the 2nd melody in "Everywhere the Beautiful", "Kenya the Beautiful" should first be sung strongly (after "Russia the Beautiful") then repeated softly (as part of the harmonic foundation) while the remaining 3 melodies are being sung.

5. Kenya the Beautiful (Melody 2)

(from "Little Machines")

Secretary Michael

♩ = 76

C   G

Li - ons and cro - co - diles,   e - ven the wart - hog smiles.

G⁷   C   G⁷

Ze- bras, gi- raffes, all here in Ken - ya, the beau - ty of A - fri - ca.

C   G

Pe - li - cans spread their wings,   os - tri - ches try to sing   fla -

D⁷   G   G⁷

min- goes and cranes and par- rots with brains, we're all kinds of fea - thers sing- ing to - ge - ther.

C   G

And un - der -neath the spar- kl - ing wa - ter___ the mar- lins and dol -phins play

G⁷   C   C⁷

Tu - na fish hur - tles___ past ur- chins and tur - tles,___ past oc - to-pus and Man - ta ray.___ And

F   C

who is the ste - ward___ who keeps this in bal - ance,___ pro - tec-ting our di - ver - si - ty?

Dm⁷   G⁷   C

Ken- ya the beau - ty, Ken- ya the beau - ty,___ the keep- er of our de - sti - ny.

When sung as the 3rd melody in "Everywhere the Beautiful", "China the Beautiful"
should first be sung strongly (after "Kenya the Beautiful") then repeated softly
(as part of the harmonic foundation) while the remaining 2 melodies are being sung.

5. China the Beautiful (Melody 3)

(from "Little Machines")

Secretary Michael

The beau - ty of Chi - na, it grows a - cross the cen - tu - ries. From fer - tile Yel - low Ri - ver plain, the com - mon strug - gle still sus - tains the beau - ty of Chi - na from Yun - nan jun - gle to the Go - bi sands. May Yang - tze's course re - main a source of peace and beau - ty to all of Man.

Yellow River Plain: the basin of the Yellow River is considered the cradle of Chinese Civilization
Yunnan: the southern province that borders Laos; famous for its great biological (and cultural) diversity
Yangtze: refers to the Yangtze River, the longest river in Asia (and the 3rd-longest in the world)
Gobi: refers to the cold Gobi Desert, the largest desert in Asia (and the 5th-largest in the world)

When sung as the 4th melody in "Everywhere the Beautiful", "Cuba the Beautiful"
should first be sung strongly (after "China the Beautiful") then repeated softly
(as part of the harmonic foundation) during the final melody ("America the Beautiful").

5. Cuba the Beautiful (Melody 4)

(from "Little Machines")

Secretary Michael

♩ = 76

The beau-ty is a-live in Cu - ba,___ from co-ral reef to moun-tain top,___ from

dark-est cave to spar-k'ling wet - lands___ our beau-ty ne-ver ne-ver stops! The

fish and wild-life thrive in Cu-ba,___ from hum-ming-birds to paint-ed snails, from

ti - ny bats to crabs and tur - tles,___ from cro-co-diles to sharks and whales. The

beau-ty is a-live in Cu - ba,___ pro - tec-ted by di-ver-si-ty,___ an

is-land that is clean and heal - thy,___ the way the earth would want to be.___ The

beau-ty is a-live in Cu-ba,___ we live it e - v'ry sin-gle day.___ En -

vi - ro-men-tal re - vo-lu - tion!___ And Cu-ba we will lead the way!___

This is the final melody sung in "Everywhere the Beautiful". While it is being sung strongly, the other melodies are being sung softly (as a harmonic foundation).

5. America the Beautiful (Melody 5)

(from "Little Machines")

Katharine Lee Bates, c.1893 *(adapted)*   Samuel A Ward, c.1882 *(adapted)*

Write Your Own "Everywhere the Beautiful" Melody

"Everywhere the Beautiful" was conceived of as an international song containing many different melodies with many different lyrics sung in many different languages at the same time. But if all the tunes are to fit nicely on top of each other without fighting, they all have to follow the same chord chart. Secretary Michael used "America the Beautiful" as the model for creating the "Everywhere the Beautiful" chord chart.

Secretary Michael only prepared scores for 5 countries - there are about 190 more to do. If you want a different one, you'll have to create it yourself. The above guide should be helpful.

The notes on the staves show the possible pitches you can choose if you want to stay on the right chord. The more your melody strays from these notes, the muddier things will sound when all the melodies are combined together. If followed strictly, there is no limit to the number of melodies that can be sung simultaneously.

Normally a little mud is okay. In fact, when Samuel Ward wrote the music to "America the Beautiful" back in 1882, he wrote 11 notes that don't fit our chord chart. That's 11 pieces of mud that you'll have to work around from the get-go. The more non-chordal notes you add, the more complicated the puzzle becomes. But it can be done!

6. Friend of Time

(from "Little Machines")

Secretary Michael

(4 seconds per measure)

Upper

Middle

Lower
*(mixed oct-
aves okay)*

Tick-Tock, Tick-Tock,

Time, Time, Friend of Time. Time, Time, Friend of Time. Time, Time,

Time, Time, Friend of Time. Time, Time,

Tick-Tock, Tick-Tock, Tick-Tock, Tick-Tock, Tick-Tock, Tick-Tock, I am a Friend of

Friend of Time. Time, Time, Friend of Time. Time, Time,

Friend of Time. Time, Time, Friend of Time. Time, Time,

*repeat final 8 bars as often as desired;
with 1 repeat, the song lasts 1min 40sec;
each additional repeat adds 32 seconds;*

Time._____ I am a Friend of Time._____ Time.

Friend of Time. Time, Time, Friend of Time. Time.

Friend of Time. Time, Time, Friend of Time. Time.

7. Great Circles

(from "Little Machines")

Ada R Habershon, 1907

Secretary Michael
Charles H Gabriel , 1907

Middle Voices: May our cir - cles be un - bro ken by and by and by and by. May they

Upper Voices / M: reach out 'round the world__ like a calm and__ peace - ful sky. From

U: right here where we're stand- ing, Great Cir - cles reach and reach. They

Lower Voices: Right where we're stand - ing Great Cir - cles, Great Cir - cles they

U: reach out past the moun - tain, they reach out past the beach. Con -

L: reach past the moun - tain they reach past the beach.___ Con -

U: nect - ing all the wo - men, con - nect - ing all the men. Great

L: nect - ing the wo - men con - nect - ing the men the Great

26

In Geometry, a "great circle" refers to a circle on a sphere in which the plane containing the circle passes through the center of the sphere (such as earth's equator and earth's lines of longitude). Therefore a person can stand as a pole and have countless great circles emanate in all directions around the earth.

8. How High Can We Go?

(from "Little Machines")

Secretary Michael
Wolfgang Amadeus Mozart, 1791

11

Bm / Em

how high, how high, how high can we go?   Want to know__

work and work and work and work and work and work and work and work and

How low, how low, how low can we go?

13

C

how high, how high, how high can we go?   Want to know__

work and work and work and work and work and work and work and work and

How low, how low, how low can we go?

15

G / D7 / G / C

how high, how high, how high, how high, how up in the sky high can we

work and work and work and work and work and work and work and work and

On - ly thing we want to know:

17

G / C / G / Em

how up in the sky high can we go?   Want to

work and work and work and work and work and work and work and work and

How low, how low, how low can we, how low can we,

30

27
G C G C
how up in the sky high can we how up in the sky high can we
work and work and work and work and work and work and work and work and
want to know: How low, how low,
29
G Em C C♯o7
go? We want to know how
work and work and work and work and work and work and work and work and
how low can we, how low can we, how low can we?
31
G Em D D7
high, how high can we
work and work and work and work and work and work and work and work and
On - ly want to know:
33
G
go?
work and work and work and work and work.
How low can we go?

32

Notes

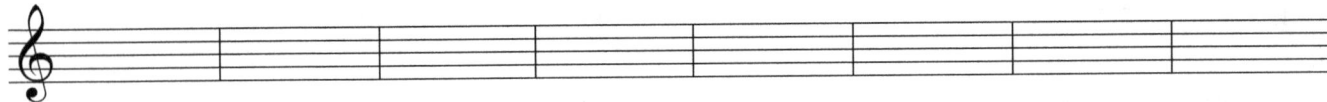

9

17

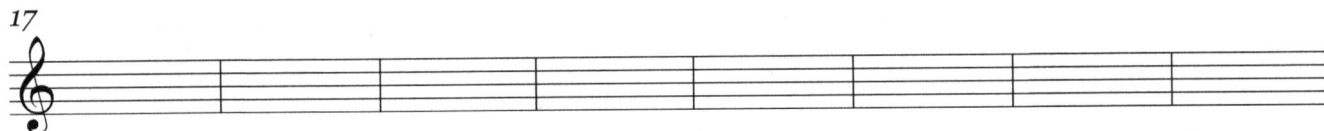

25

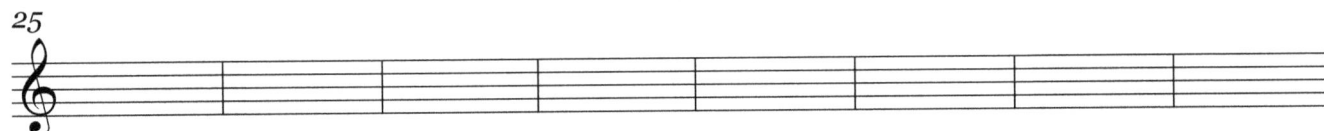

33

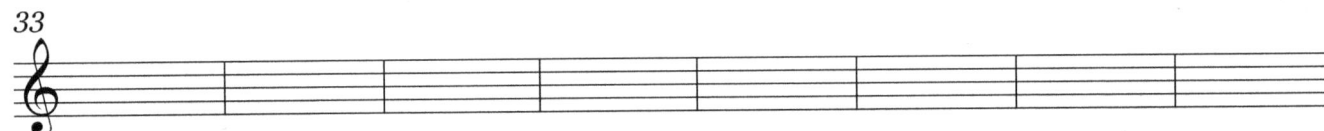

41

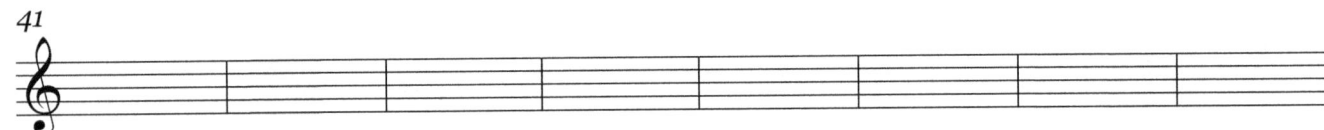

49

57

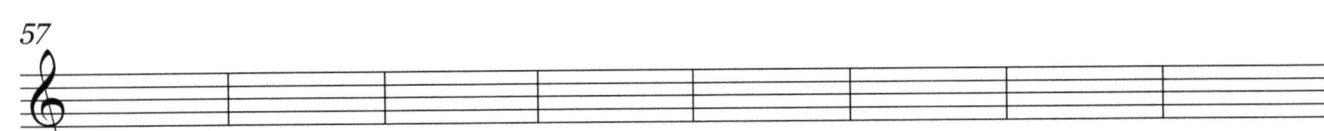

9. I am a Machine

(from "Little Machines")

Secretary Michael

Directions: Voice 1 begins alone at section 1. When voice 1 reaches section 2, Voice 2 begins at the beginning of the song. When voice 1 reaches section 3, voice 3 begins at the beginning of the song. (If Voice 1 sings through the entire song 3 times, then Voice 2 will have sung through it 2 2/3 times and Voice 3 will have sung through it 2 1/3 times.) To end the song, everybody sings the alternate notes for "SERENE" (written with capital letters and a small dotted-half note).

Chugging Along ♩. = 63

Section 1

Dmin — G

Beep beep beep beep beep Beep beep beep beep beep

3 Dmin — G

Beep beep beep beep beep Beep beep beep beep beep
SE - RENE.

Section 2

5 Dmin — G

I am a ma - chine._____

7 Dmin — G

My life is se - rene.
SE - RENE.

Section 3

IMPORTANT: Accents are with the beats, not with the syllables

9 Dmin — G

CHUG - a chug - A chug - a CHUG - a chug - A chug - a

repeat as needed, eventually ending together on the word "serene"

11 Dmin — G

CHUG - a chug - A chug - a CHUG - a chug - A chug - a
SE - RENE.

10. I See Your Differences and I Smile

(from "Little Machines")

Secretary Michael

With a Smile ♩ = 63

I see your dif-fren-ces. I see your

D

Smile. Dif-fren-ces, I see your dif-fren-ces,

Smile._____ Dif- fer, dif-fer, dif-fer, dif-fer, dif-fer, dif-fer. Dif- fer, dif-fer, dif-fer

F   Bb   Gmin

dif - fren - ces. I see your dif - fren - ces and I

I see your dif - fren - ces, I see your
(and I)

dif - fer, dif - fer, dif - fer. Dif - fer, dif - fer, dif - fer dif - fer, dif - fer, dif - fer.

1.   Repeat   2.
A   D   as desired   A   D

smile._____ smile,_____ I____ smile.

dif fren-ces, and I Smile. Smile, I smile.

Dif- fer, dif - fer, dif - fer Smile._____ Smile, I smile.

Notes

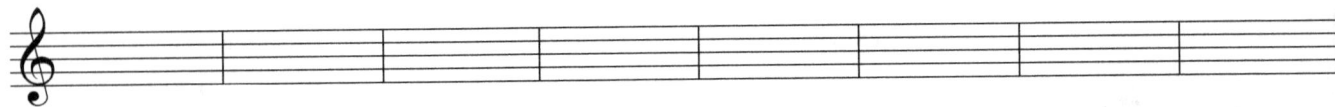

9

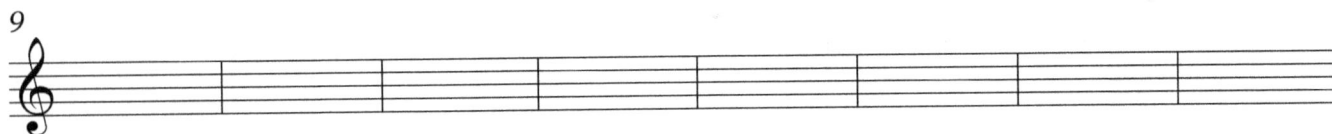

17

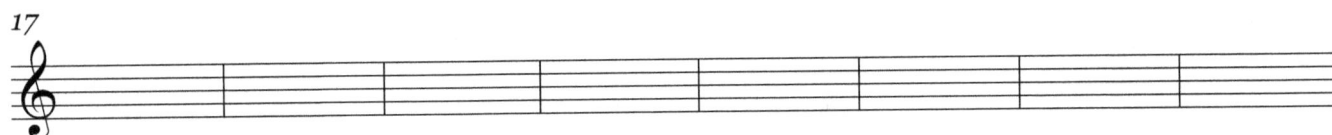

25

33

41

49

57

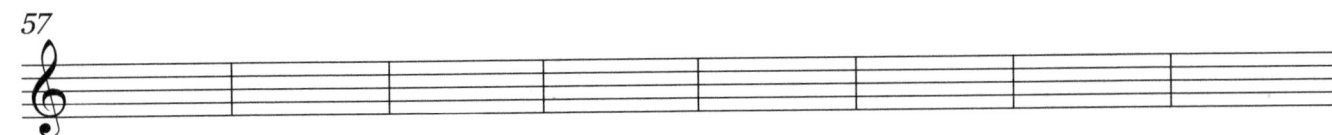

11. Interval Round

(from "Little Machines")

Directions: Voice 1 begins alone at Section 1. When Voice 1 reaches Section 2, Voice 2 begins at the beginning of the song. When Voice 1 reaches Section 3, Voice 3 begins at the beginning of the song. (If Voice 1 sings through the entire song 3 times, then Voice 2 will have sung through it 2 2/3 times and Voice 3 will have sung through it 2 1/3 times.) A nice way to end the song is for everybody to sing the word "HARMONY", blending on an "A" chord (A-C#-E)

Secretary Michael

12. Keep Us Open

(from "Little Machines")

Secretary Michael

Repeat as often as desired

21 | A♭   E♭   B♭

Keep the world the whole wide world our fa - mi - ly.

keep the world our fa - mi - ly.

Keep the world our fa - mi - ly.

ENDING SECTION

25 | E♭   B♭6   B♭7   Cm   Gaug   A♭

Keep us o - pen, keep us free,__ keep the world our fa - mi - ly__ Keep the world the

Keep us o - pen, keep us free,__ keep the world our fa - mi - ly__ keep the

Keep us o - pen, keep us free, Keep the world our fa - mi - ly. Keep the

30 | A♭Maj7   B♭7   E♭

whole wide world our fa - - mi - Keep us o - pen keep us free.

world our fa - - mi - - ly.____

world our fa - - mi - - ly.____

Notes

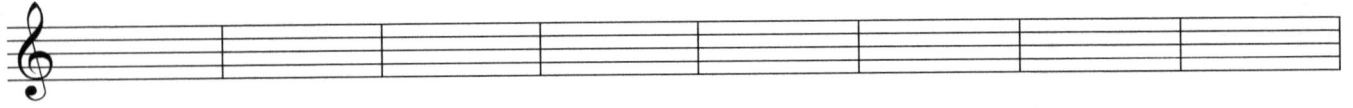

9

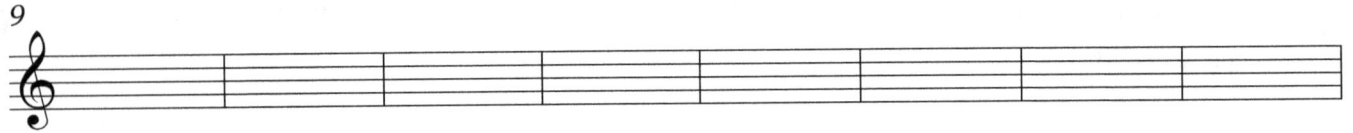

17

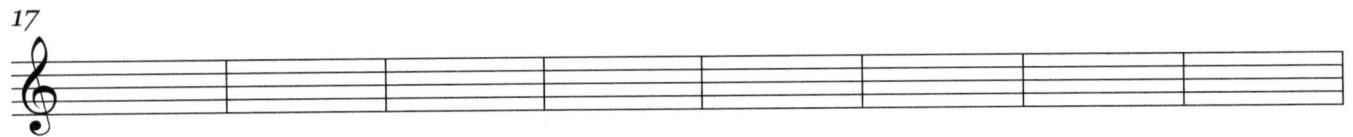

25

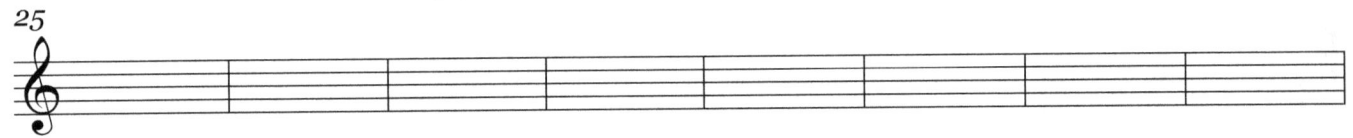

33

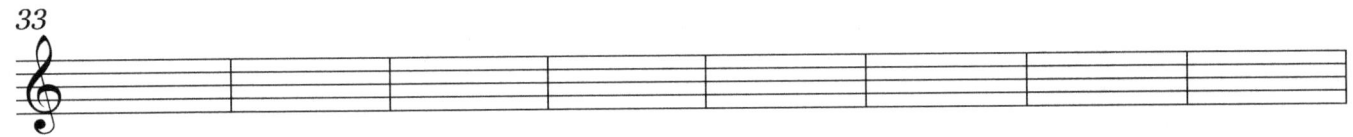

41

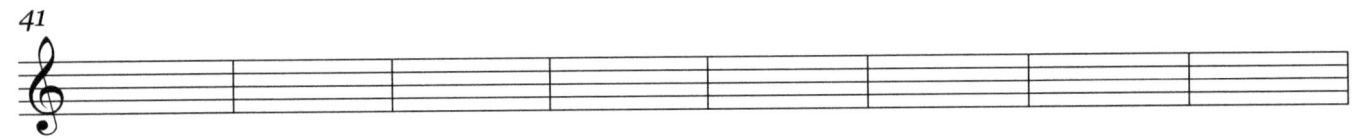

49

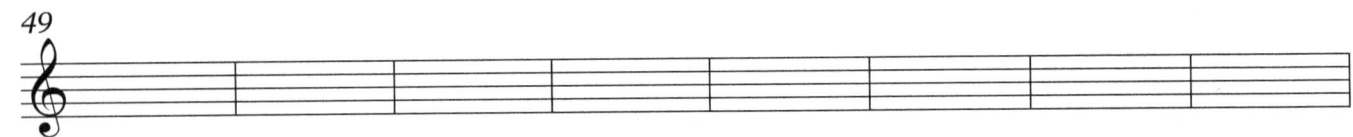

57

13. Live, Let Live

(from "Little Machines")

Secretary Michael

Slow, Meditative

♪ = 102

Upper

Middle

Live — let live — let Live — let live — let

Lower

Live,— let live. Live,— let live. Live,— let live. Live,— let live.

Live,— let live.— Live— let live.— Live— let live.—

Live — let live — let Live — let live — let Live — let live — let

Live,— let live. Live,— let live. Live,— let live.

Repeat as desired

Live,— let live.— Live,— let live.— Let— live.—

Live — let live — let Live — let live. Let— live.—

Live,— let live. Live,— let live. Live,— let live.—

14. Marching to the Future

(from "Little Machines")

Secretary Michael

Essential Accompaniment:
An army of marching feet (in quarter notes) begins 2 bars before voices, continuing to end of song.

♩ = 60

Middle: March ing, march ing, march ing, march ing, march ing, march ing, march ing, marching

Lower (as written and octave lower): March, march, marching march. March, march, march ing march. March, march, march ing march.

4

Upper: March - ing to the fu - ture,____ to the peo - ple we will meet. We are

Middle: March - ing, march - ing, march - ing, march - ing, march - ing, march- ing, march - ing, march - ing.

Lower: March, march, march - ing march. March, march, march - ing march.

6

March - ing to the fu - ture,____ to the peo - ple we will meet. May we

March - ing, march - ing, march - ing, march - ing, march - ing, march - ing, march - ing, march - ing.

March, march, march - ing march. March, march, march - ing march.

8 F   C

ne - ver have a vic - to - ry. May we

March - ing, march - ing, march - ing, march - ing, march - ing, march - ing. Vic - to - ry!

March - ing, march - ing, march - ing, march - ing, march - ing march. Vic - to - ry!

PD *All works by Secretary Michael have been placed in the Public Domain. They may be freely copied and performed.*

10

ne - ver have a vic - to - ry. May we

March - ing, march - ing, march - ing, march - ing, march - ing, march - ing. Vic - to - ry!

March - ing, march - ing, march - ing, march - ing, march - ing march. Vic - to - ry!

12

ne - ver have a vic - to - ry. May we

March - ing, march - ing, march - ing, march - ing, march - ing, march - ing. Vic - to - ry!

March - ing, march - ing, march - ing, marcy - ing, march - ing, march. Vic - to - ry!

14 Dmin   G   G⁷

smile at our de - -

March - ing, march - ing, march - ing, march - ing. March - ing, march - ing, march - ing, march - ing.

March - ing, march - ing, march - ing, march - ing. March - ing, march - ing, march - ing, march - ing.

(Repeat as often as desired using this measure,
but at end of song use "ending 2" instead.)

16 1.   2.

March - ing to the fu - ture, to the   March - ing to the fu - ture, to the peo - ple we will meet.

feat. *(Thank you, middle voices, for*   feat.
completing the upper voices' phrase.)

March, march, march - ing march.   March, march, march - ing march.   March, march, march.

44

15. Mud to Flower

(from "Little Machines")

Secretary Michael

17 mud_____ to flow - er_____ back to mud_____ then

_____ to flow - er to flow - er_____ to flow - er_____

Mud_____ to Mud_____ to Mud_____ to

20 flow er_____ our_ gar - den needs_____ them both.

_____ to flow er_____ to flow er_____ to flow er._____

Mud_____ to Mud_____ to Mud_____ to Mud.

25 Lower Voice

Pain_____ to Pain_____ to Pain_____ to Pain_____ to

29 Middle Voice

to Joy_____ to Joy_____ to Joy_____

Lower Voice

Pain_____ to Pain_____ to Pain_____ to

32
C#o D C#o D C#o D
U
From pain, to joy, back to pain, then joy, the back and
M
to Joy to Joy to Joy to Joy to Joy to Joy
L
Pain to Pain to Pain to Pain to Pain to Pain to
38
C#o D C#o D C#o
forth of growth. From pain to joy, back to
to Joy to Joy to Joy to Joy to Joy
Pain to Pain to Pain to Pain to Pain to
43
D C#o D C#o D
pain, then joy, our gar - den needs them both.
to Joy to Joy to Joy to Joy
Pain to Pain to Pain to Pain to Pain.

16. Popcorn Waltz

(from "Little Machines")

Secretary Michael
Johann Strauss, Jr, 1867

Rich, melted-cheese legato
9
C
pop pop pop. Pop - Pop, Pop - Pop. Pop pop pop
14
G7
pop. Pop - Pop, Pop - Pop. Pop pop pop pop. Pop -
19
C
Pop, Pop - Pop. Pop pop pop pop. Pop - Pop, Pop -

24
C7
Pop. Pop pop pop pop. Pop - Pop, Pop - Pop. Pop pop pop
30
F
Dm
G7
pop. Pop - Pop, Pop - Pop. Pop pop pop pop, pop pop
36
C
Dm
G7
C
pop, pop pop pop pop pop pop pop. Pop - Pop.

17. Somewhere There's a Place

(from "Little Machines")

Secretary Michael
Johannes Pachelbel, c. 1694

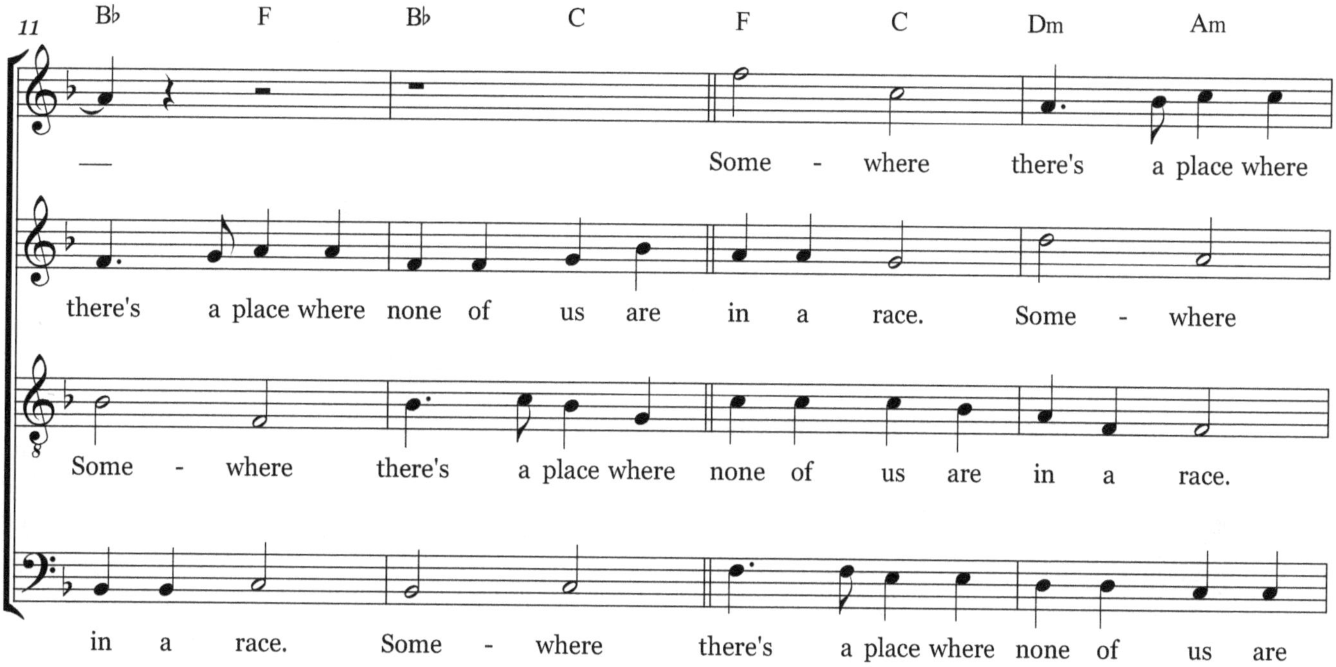
11
B♭ F B♭ C F C Dm Am
Some - where there's a place where
there's a place where none of us are in a race. Some - where
Some - where there's a place where none of us are in a race.
in a race. Some - where there's a place where none of us are

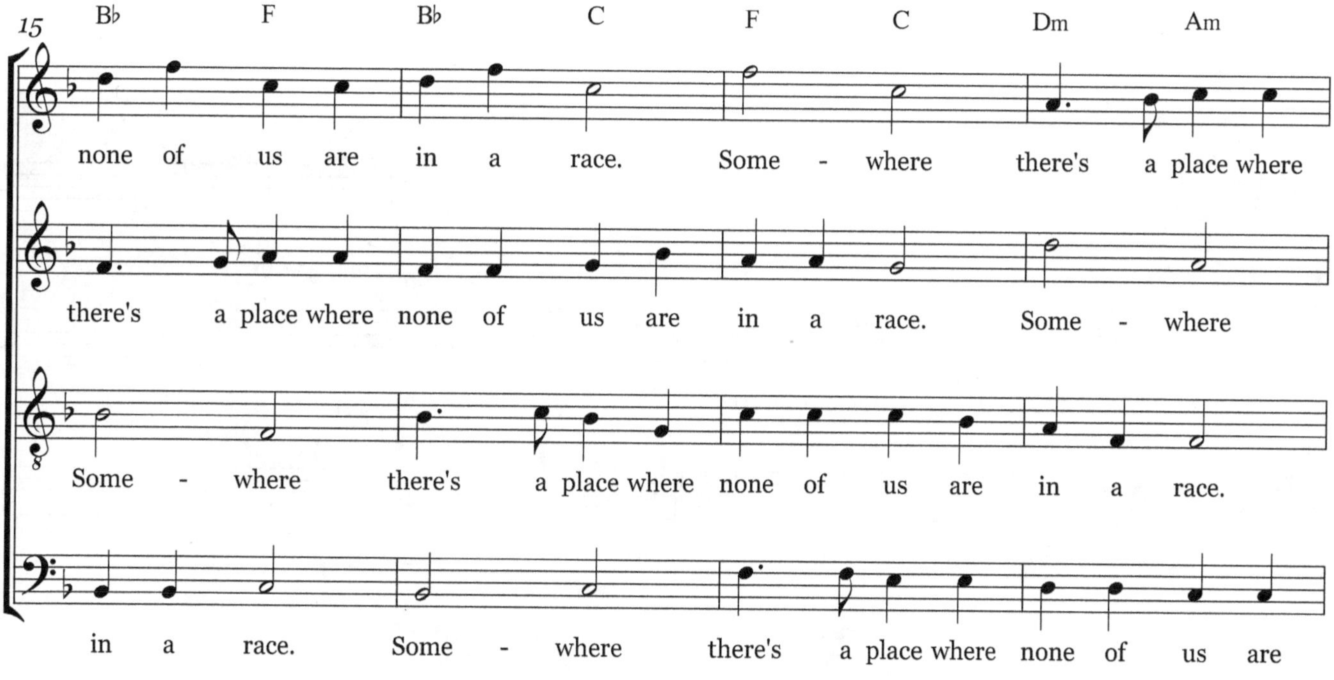
15
B♭ F B♭ C F C Dm Am
none of us are in a race. Some - where there's a place where
there's a place where none of us are in a race. Some - where
Some - where there's a place where none of us are in a race.
in a race. Some - where there's a place where none of us are

19

Bb F Bb C F C Dm Am

none of us are in a race. Some - where Some - where

there's a place where none of us are Some - where

Some - where there's a place where

in a race. Some - where

23

Bb F Bb C Bb C⁷ F

there's a place.

Some_ where_ there's a place.

Some - where Some - where there's a place.

Some - where there's a place.

Notes

9

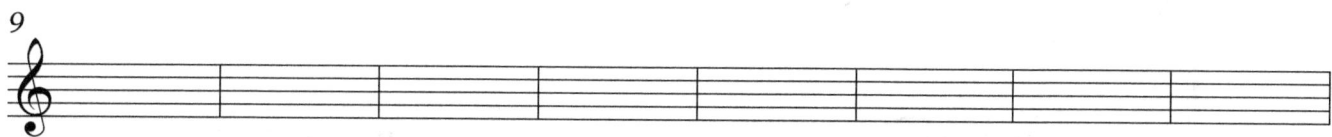

17

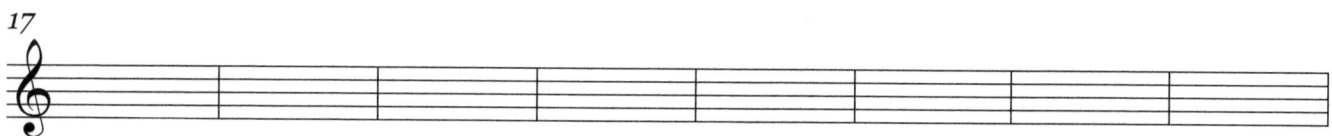

25

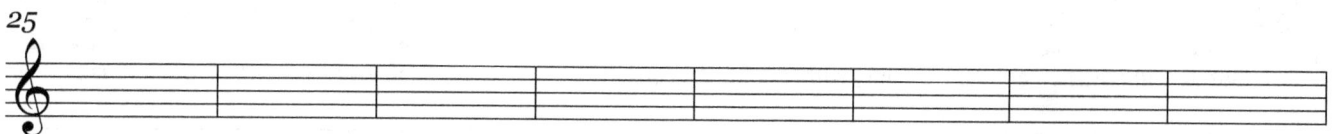

33

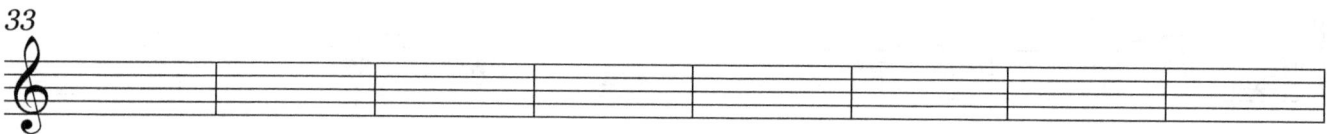

41

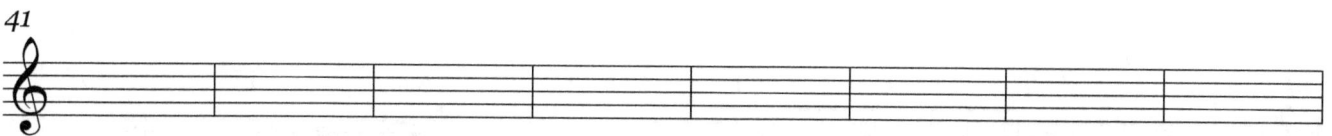

49

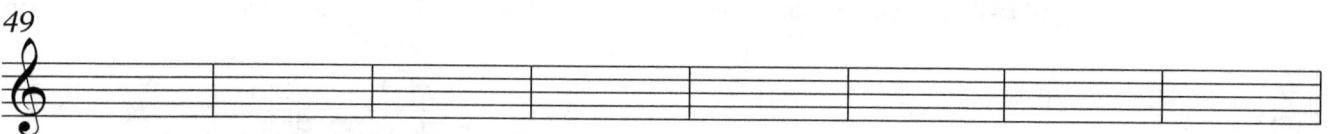

57

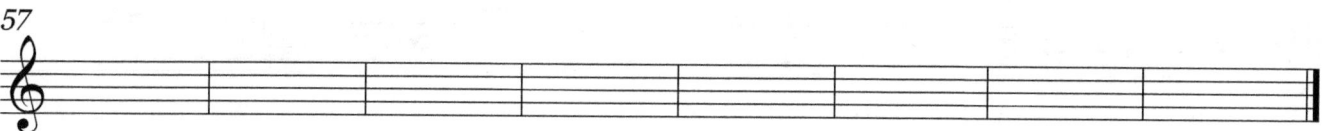

18. Suffering is a Part of Life

(from "Little Machines")

Secretary Michael

Melody

Whistlers

Moaners

Woe__ Woe__ Woe, Woe, Woe__ Woe__ Woe__ Woe, Woe, Woe_

Suf-fer-ing is__ a part of life, with pain, fru-stra-tion and loss of loved ones. Suf-fer-ing is__ a

Woe_____ Woe_____ Woe, Woe, Woe_____ Woe_____

part of life. We whis-tle be-cause we be- long.__ Suf-fer-ing is__ a part of life, with

pulsed

(whistled)

Woe_____ Woe, Woe, Woe__ Woe_____ Woe_____

19

pain,___ fru-stra-tion and loss of loved ones.___ Suf-fer-ing is___ a part of life. We

pulsed

Woe, Woe, Woe_____ Woe_____ Woe_____

23

whis-tle be-cause we be- long._____ Suf-fer-ing is___ a part of life, with

pulsed

(whistled)

Woe, Woe, Woe_____ Woe_____ Woe_____

27

pain,___ fru-stra- tion and loss of loved ones.___ Suf-fer-ing is___ a

pulsed

Woe, Woe, Woe_____ Woe_____

30

part of life. We whis- tle be-cause we be- long._____

Woe_____ Woe, Woe, Woe_____

19. Superstition

(from "Little Machines")

Secretary Michael
Charles Gounod, 1872

10
F E A7 Dm
Ooo... Ooo... Ooo...
Tick-tock-tick. Tock-tick-tock. Tick-tock-tick. Tock-tick-tock. Tick-tock-tick. Tock-tick-tock.
night. But sci-ence turns
sti - tions bite. At night there's
13
A7 Dm A7
Ooo...
Tick-tock-tick. Tock-tick-tock. Tick-tock-tick. Tock-tick-tock. Tick-tock-tick. Tock-tick-tock.
on the light. But sci-ence turns on the light
fear. At night there's fright. At
16
Dm A7 Dm C F E
Ooo... Ooo... Ooo...
Tick-tock-tick. Tock-tick-tock. Tick-tock-tick. Tock-tick-tock. Tick-tock-tick. Tock-tick-tock.
to chase the fear, to chase the fright, to chase the
night the su - per - sti - tions

19 A⁷ / Dm / A⁷

Ooo... / Ooo...

Tick - tock - tick. Tock - tick - tock. Tick - tock - tick. Tock - tick - tock. Tick - tock - tick. Tock - tick - tock.

things that go bump in the night. But sci - ence turns on the light.

bite. At night there's fear._____ At

22 Dm / A⁷ / Dm C/E

Ooo... / Ooo...

Tick - tock - tick. Tock - tick - tock. Tick - tock - tick. Tock - tick - tock. Tick - tock - tick. Tock - tick - tock.

But sci - ence turns on the light to chase the

night there's fright._____ At night the

25 F Eb / Dm A⁷ / Dm

Ooo... / Ooo... / Bright.

Tick - tock - tick. Tock - tick - tock. Tick - tock - tick. Tock - tick - tock. Tick - tock - tick. Bright.

fear,__ and fright__ un - til__ the truth shines bright.

su - per - sti - tions bite.

Notes

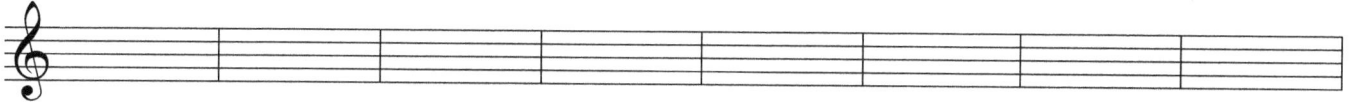

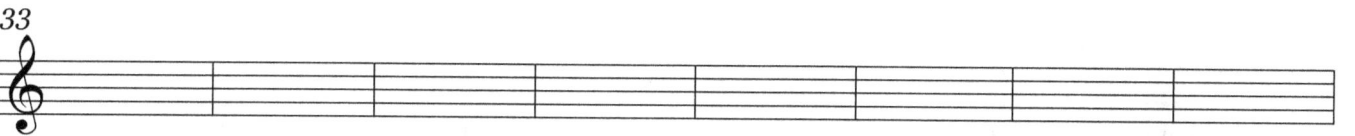

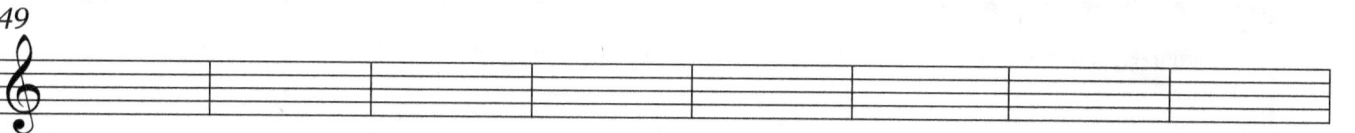

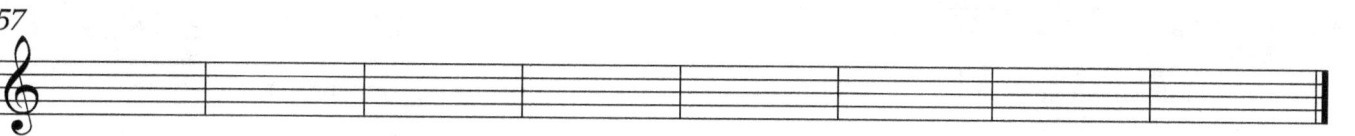

20. Taking Off My Jersey

(from "Little Machines")

Secretary Michael

♩ = 88

V1: Tak-ing off my jer-sey I feel ligh-ter. Tak-ing off my jer-sey, I feel ligh-ter.

V1: Sud-den-ly my world is so much brigh ter. Tak-ing off my jer-sey, I feel light, light, light. I am

V1: float - - ing. I am float - - ing.
V2: Tak-ing off my jer-sey, I feel ligh - ter. Tak-ing off my jer-sey, I feel ligh - ter.

V1: Sud-den ly my world is so much brigh ter. Tak-ing off my jer-sey, I feel light, light, light, takes me
V2: Sud-den ly my world is so much brigh ter. Tak-ing off my jer-sey, I feel light, light, light, I am

V1: High-er___ and high-er___ and high er,___ and high-er, takes me high-er___ and high-er___ and
V2: float - - ing. I am float - -
V3: Tak-ing off my jer-sey takes me high - er. Tak-ing off my jer-sey takes me

20
Emin
Amin
D
V1
high- er, and high-er high-er takes me to the place that I a - spire, a- spire For
V2
ing. Takes me to the place that I a - spire.
V3
high - er. Takes me to the place that I a - spire.
23
Amin
D
G
V1
tak-ing off my jer-sey takes me high, high, high-er, high-er High-er than the walls be-tween the
V2
Tak-ing off my jer-sey takes me high, high, high-er takes me High-er and high-er and
V3
Tak-ing off my jer-sey takes me high, high, high. I am float - - -
26
Emin
G
Emin
V1
peo - ple. High er than the flag-pole and the stee - ple.
V2
high er, and high-er, takes me high-er and high-er and high er, and high-er. Takes me
V3
ing. I am float - - - ing.
29
Amin
D
Amin
V1
Way up here a-bove the them and us - 's. Way up here a-mong the peace ful
V2
way up here a-bove the them and us-'s, them and us-'s. way up here a-mong the peace ful
V3
Way up here a-bove the them and us - 's. Way up here a-mong the peace ful

32
D
G
Emin
V1
cu - mu - lu - ses, I am float - - - ing. I am
V2
cu - mu - lu - ses, takes me High-er than the walls be-tween the peo - ple.
V3
cu - mu - lu - ses, takes me High-er___ and high-er___ and high-er,___ and high-er, takes me
35
G
Emin
Amin
V1
float - - - ing. Way up here a-bove the them and
V2
High-er than the flag-pole and the stee - ple. Way up here a-bove the them and
V3
high-er___ and high-er___ and high er,___ and high-er. Takes me way up here a-bove the them and
38
D
Amin
D
V1
us - 's. Way up here a-mong the peace ful cu - mu - lu - ses, takes me
V2
us - 's. Way up here a-mong the peace ful cu - mu - lu - ses. I am
V3
us - 's, them and us - 's.___ way up here a-mong the peace ful cu - mu - lu - ses.

Repeat is optional; (Time with repeat: 3'23" / Time without repeat: 2'15")

21. Tiny Change Yodel

(from "Little Machines")

Secretary Michael

Lyrics:
A ti - ny, ti - ny change. A change the world can see. A

ti - ny, ti - ny change. The change___ is me. A

ti - ny, ti - ny change. A change the world can see. A

Ti - ny change, world can see.

14

G   C   D7   G   A

ti - ny, ti - ny change. The change___ is me. A

Ti - ny change. The change is me.

(In yodeling, the voice jumps up and down between a lower pitch and an upper pitch; the lower pitch is sung with a "normal" voice, but the upper pitch is purposely sung above the voice's break - in the "head voice" or falsetto register)

18

G   C   G   D7

ti - ny, ti - ny, ti - ny, ti - ny, ti - ny, ti - ny, ti - ny, ti - ny, ti - ny change. A___

ti - ny, ti - ny change. A change the world can see. A

Ti - ny change, world can see.

1.   2.

22

G   C   D7   G   G

ti - ny, ti - ny, ti - ny, ti - ny, ti - ny, ti - ny, ti - ny, ti - ny, ti - ny change. A___ change.

ti - ny, ti - ny change. The change___ is me. A me.

Ti - ny change. The change is me. me.

22. Traveling Heals

(from "Little Machines")

Secretary Michael
Roud #23650

♩=72

Soprano Response: Tra-ve-ling heals. Tra-ve-ling heals. Tra-ve-ling heals. Tra-ve-ling heals. Tra-ve-ling heals. Tra-ve-ling

Alto Counter-Melody: If tra-vel pro-tects— the mind from ha-tred and tra-vel builds trust by what it re-veals, then may the whole world have free-dom to tra-vel, for

Bass Call: Tra-ve-ling heals. Tra-ve-ling heals. Tra-ve-ling heals. Tra-ve-ling heals. Tra-ve-ling heals. Tra-ve-ling heals. Tra-ve-ling heals. Tra-ve-ling heals. Tra-ve-ling heals.

Chords: F C F C Dm Gm G⁷ C F C F C

19
Dm
Gm
F
Soprano Response
heals. Tra - ve - ling, tra - ve - ling heals.
Alto Counter-Melody
tra - ve-ling, tra - ve - ling, tra - ve - ling heals. If tra - vel pro -
Tenor Melody
If tra - vel pro -
Bass Call
Tra - ve - ling heals. Tra - ve - ling heals. Tra - ve - ling
24
C
F
C
Dm
Gm
G7
Tra - ve - ling heals. Tra - ve - ling heals. Tra - ve - ling heals.
tects_ the mind from ha - tred and tra - vel builds trust by what it re -
tects_ the mind_ from ha - tred and tra - vel builds trust_ by what it re -
heals. Tra - ve - ling heals. Tra - ve - ling heals. Tra - ve - ling

30

C   F   C   F   C

Tra - ve - ling   heals.   Tra - ve - ling   heals.   Tra - ve - ling

veals,   then   may   the whole world   have   free - dom to   tra - vel,   for

veals,   then   may   the whole world   have   free - dom to   tra - vel,   for

heals.   Tra - ve - ling   heals.   Tra - ve - ling   heals.

35

Dm   Gm   C   **1.** F   **2.** F

heals.   Tra - ve - ling,   tra - ve - ling   heals.   heals.

tra - ve - ling,   tra - ve - ling,   tra - ve - ling   heals.   If   heals.

tra - ve - ling,   tra - ve - ling,   tra - ve - ling   heals.   If   heals.

Tra - ve - ling   heals.   Tra - ve - ling   heals.   heals.

23. Troubled Child

(from "Little Machines")

Secretary Michael
(ancient melody)

♪=92

Trou - bled child, trou - bled child, what do we do with our trou___ bled child?

Trou - bled child, trou - bled child, what do we do with our trou - bled child?

Trou - bled child, trou - bled child, what do we do with our trou___ bled child?

Trou - bled child, trou - bled child, what do we do with our trou - bled child?

Trou - bled child, trou - bled child, what do we do with our trou - bled child?

Trou - bled child, trou - bled child, what do we do with our trou - bled child?

Could be a girl or could be a boy who fills us with fear in - stead of joy.

Could be a girl, could be a boy, fills us with fear in - stead of joy.

21
G D Bm C B E(sus4) Em
U
Lock them a - way? Or let them run wild? Oh what do we do with our trou - bled child?
M
What
L
Lock them a - way? Let them run wild? What do we do with our trou - bled child?
25
Em G D Bm Em Am B
U
Trou - bled child, trou - bled child, what do we do with our trou__ bled child?
M
child is this who laid to rest__ on mo - ther's lap____ is sleep - ing? And
L
Trou - bled child, trou - bled child, what do we do with our trou - bled child?
29
Em G D Bm Em B
U
Trou - bled child, trou - bled child, what do we do with our
M
who are we____ if we can't see____ a hap - py, heal - thy
L
Trou - bled child, trou - bled child, what do we do with our

32
E(sus4) Em G D Bm
U
trou - bled child? Could be a girl or could be a boy who
M
be - ing? Hey! Hey! let's clear the way for the
L
trou - bled child? Could be a girl, could be a boy,
35
Em Am B G
U
fills us with fear in - stead of joy. Lock them a - way? Or
M
fu - ture we are see - ing. Hey! Hey! let's
L
fills us with fear in - stead of joy. Lock them a - way?
38
D Bm C B E(sus4) Em
U
let them run wild? Oh what do we do with our trou - bled child?
M
clear the way for a hap - py, heal - thy be - ing.
L
Let them run wild? What do we do with our trou - bled child?

Notes

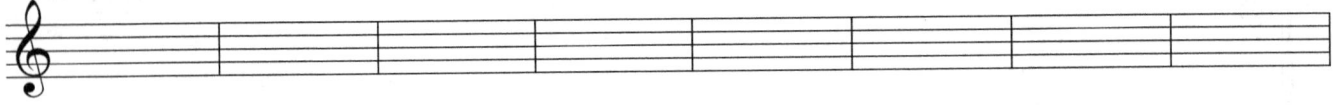

9

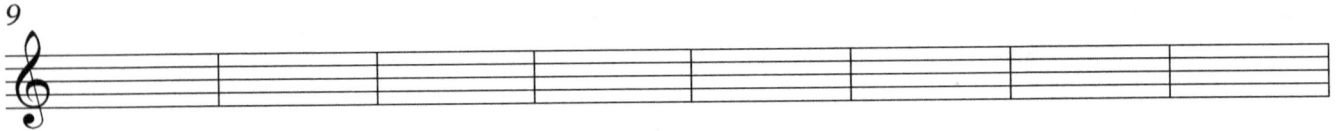

17

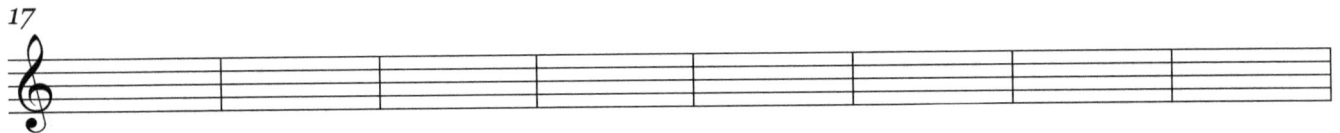

25

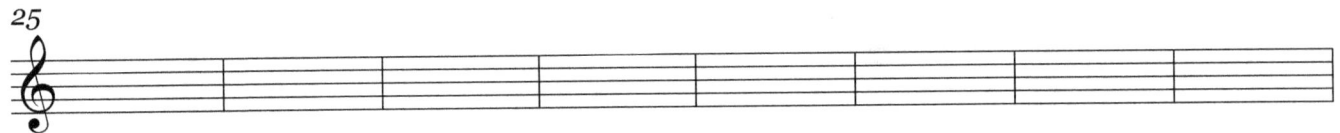

33

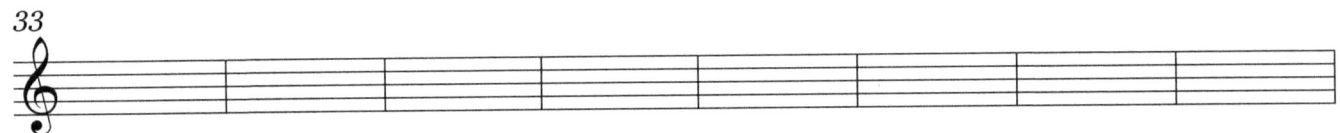

41

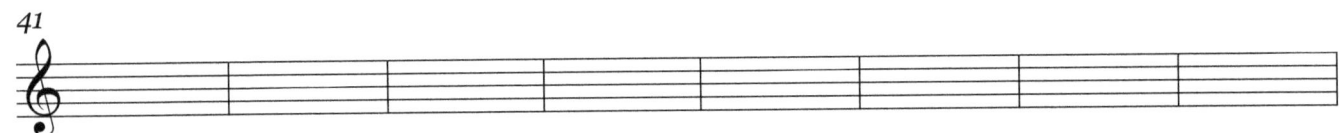

49

57

24. Tuning to Each Other

(from "Little Machines")

Secretary Michael

25. Up-Down Polka

(from "Little Machines")

Secretary Michael

Ups: Up Up Up Up Up Up Up Up Up Up Up Up Up ...etc.

Melody: Are we go-ing up? Or are we go-ing down? Or are we stay-ing where we are just spin-ning 'roun and 'roun? May-be there's no up and may-be there's no down. May-be there's just here and now and

Downs: Down Down Down Down Down Down Down Down Down Down Down Down Down Down Down Down Down Down ...etc.

10
E7 A C#m E E7 A
Gid-dy
spin-ning 'roun and 'roun. May-be there's just here and now and spin-ning 'roun and 'roun. We
13
E Am
up, gid - dy up, gid - dy up, gid - dy up, gid - dy UP in - to the sky. Gid - dy
up and up and up and up and UP in - to the sky. We
Sky
15
E Am
up, gid - dy up, gid - dy up, gid - dy up, gid - dy UP but don't know why.
up and up and up and up and UP but don't know why. Up -
Why

17
Dm Am E Am Dm Am
Up to up a - bove. Up from those we love. Up from e - v'ry - day.
up to up a - bove. Up - up from those we love. Up - up from e - v'ry day. We
Up to up a - bove. Up from those we love. Up from e - v'ry - day.
20
E A
Up and up our lives a - way. Up Up Up Up Up Up
up and up our lives a - way. Are we go - ing up? Or
Up and up our lives a - way. Down Down Down Down
23
D C♯m E E7 A
Up Up Up Up ...etc.
are we go - ing down? Or are we stay-ing where we are just spin-ning 'roun and 'roun?
Down Down Down Down Down Down ...etc.

26
A
D
C#m
E
May - be there's no up and may - be there's no down.
May - be there's just here and now and
29
E7
A
C#m
E
spin - ning 'roun and 'roun.
Up Up Up Up
May - be there's just here and now and
Down Down Down Down
31
E7
A
spin - ning 'roun and 'round.
Up Up Up Up Up!
spin - ning 'roun and 'round.
spin - ning 'roun and
Down Down Down Down Down
Down!

26. Working

(from "Little Machines")

Secretary Michael
American Folksong, pre-1894

All works by Secretary Michael have been placed in the Public Domain. They may be freely copied and performed.

17

Sop. F
farm the land and grow the food, and work is what I do. It

Ten.
Work-ing and work ing, I work in a store, clean-ing the toi lets and mop-ping the floor.

Bass
Work - ing, work - ing, work - ing, work-ing, work - ing, work - ing, work - ing, work ing,

21

F · Dm · G⁷ · C
ain't much fun but I gets it done to feed both me and you. I

Work-ing and work ing, can be some-thing good.
Gets kind of bor-ing but it's un-der-stood:

Work - ing, work - ing, work - ing, work ing, work - ing, work - ing, work - ing, work ing,

25

Sop. F · F⁷ · B♭ · F
farm the land and grow the food, and work is what I do. It

Alto
Mel.
I've been wor - kin' on the rail - road all the live - long day.

Ten.
Work - ing and work ing, I work in a store, clean-ing the toi lets and mop-ping the floor.

Bass
Work - ing, work - ing, work - ing, work-ing, work - ing, work-ing, work - ing, work-ing,

29

F   Dm   G⁷   C

ain't much fun but I gets it done to feed both me and you. Choo! Choo! Choo!

I've been wor-kin' on the rail - road just to pass the time a - way.

Gets kind of bor-ing but it's un-der-stood: work-ing and work ing can be some-thing good.

Work - ing, work - ing, work - ing, work-ing, work - ing, work - ing, work - ing, work - ing,

33

C⁷   F   F⁷   B♭   A⁷

Can't you hear the whi-stle blo - win', rise up so ear-ly in the morn.

Can't you hear the whi-stle blo - win', rise up so ear-ly in the morn.

Can't you hear the whi-stle blo - win', rise up so ear-ly in the morn.

Work - ing, work - ing, work - ing, work - ing, work - ing, work - ing, work - ing, work - ing,

37

B♭   F   Dm   B♭⁹   C   F

Can't you hear the cap - tain shou - tin': "Di - nah blow your horn."

Can't you hear the cap - tain shou - tin': "Di - nah blow your horn."

Can't you hear the cap - tain shou - tin': "Di - nah blow your horn."

Work - ing, work - ing, work - ing, work - ing, work - ing, work - ing, work - ing, work. MELODY:

BASS

41
F
B♭
C
F
Di nah won't-cha blow, Di nah won't-cha blow, blow your horn.
Di nah won't-cha blow, Di nah won't-cha blow, blow your horn.
Di nah won't-cha blow? Di nah won't-cha blow? Di nah won't-cha blow your horn?
Di nah won't-cha blow? Di nah won't-cha blow? Di nah won't-cha blow your horn?
45
F
B♭
C
F
Di nah won't-cha blow, Di nah won't-cha blow, blow your horn. I
Di nah won't-cha blow, Di nah won't-cha blow, blow your horn.
ALTO MELODY:
Di nah won't-cha blow? Di nah won't-cha blow? Di nah won't-cha blow your horn?
Di nah won't-cha blow? Di nah won't-cha blow? Di nah won't-cha blow your horn?
49
F
F7
B♭
F
farm the land and grow the food, and work is what I do. It
I've been wor - kin' on the rail - road all the live - long day.
Work ing and work ing, I work in a store, clean ing the toi lets and mop ping the floor.
Work - ing, work - ing, work - ing, work-ing, work - ing, work - ing, work - ing, work-ing,

53
F Dm G7
ain't much fun but I gets it done to feed both me and
I've been wor - kin' on the rail - road just to pass the time a -
Gets kind of bor - ing but it's un - der - stood: work - ing and work - ing can
Work - ing, work - ing, work - ing, work - ing, work - ing, work - ing,
56
C C7 F F7
you. Work! Work! Work! May for - e - ver we be work - ing,
way. May for - e - ver we be work - ing,
be some - thing good. May for - e - ver we be work - ing,
work - ing, work - ing, Work - ing, work - ing, work - ing, work - ing,
59
B♭ A7 B♭ F Dm
for it is un - der - stood: Work - ing, work - ing, lots of work - ing
for it is un - der - stood. Work - ing, work - ing, lots of work - ing
for it is un - der - stood. Work - ing, work - ing, lots of work - ing
work - ing, work - ing, work - ing, work - ing, Work - ing, work - ing, work - ing, work - ing,

63
B♭9 C F F7 B♭ F Dm
can be some - thing good. Work - ing, work - ing, lots of work - ing
can be some - thing good. Work - ing, work - ing, lots of work - ing
can be some - thing good. Work - ing, work - ing, lots of work - ing
work - ing, work - ing, work - ing, work - ing, Work - ing, work - ing, work - ing, work - ing,
67
B♭9 C F
can be some - thing good.
can be some - thing good.
can be some - thing good.
can be some - thing work - ing, work - ing, work - ing, work.

27. Works of Art

(from "Little Machines")

Secretary Michael
Giacomo Puccini, c. 1924

Work, work, work, work, work, and sing, sing, sing, sing, sing, and

Work, work, work, work, — as works of art. Sing, sing, sing, sing, — we have a part.

Work, work, work, work, work, and sing, sing, sing, sing, sing, and

Work, work, work, work, — as works of art. Sing, — sing, — sing, — sing, —

To live our lives as works of art where all we sing-ers have a

Work, work, work, work, work, and sing, sing, sing, sing,

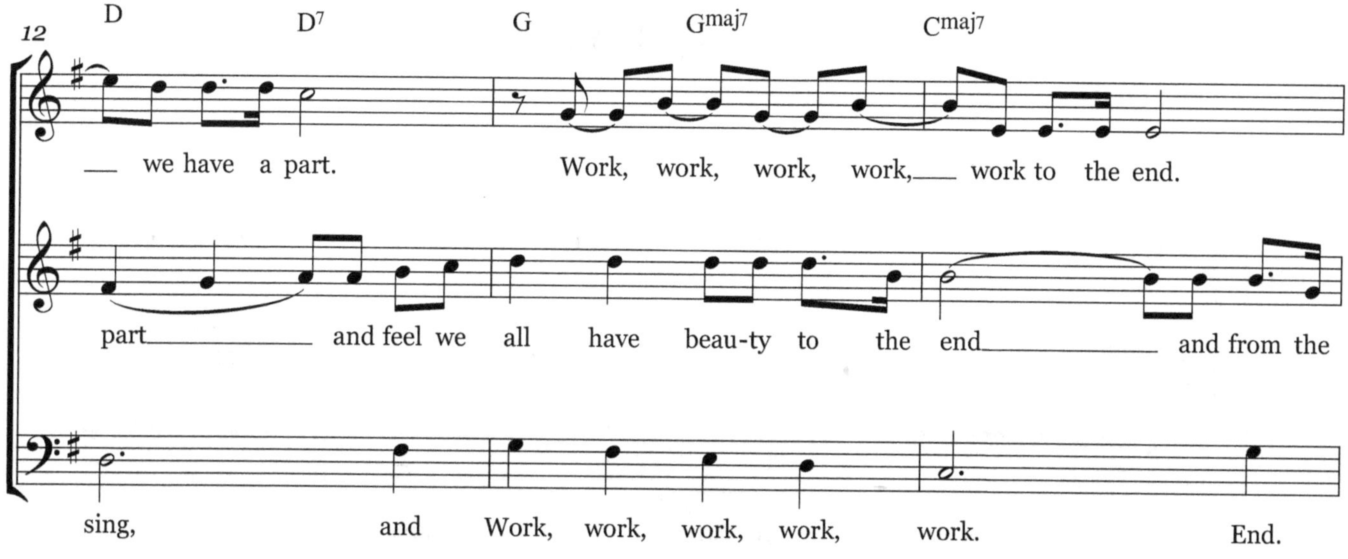
12
D D7 G Gmaj7 Cmaj7
— we have a part. Work, work, work, work,— work to the end.
part — and feel we all have beau-ty to the end — and from the
sing, and Work, work, work, work, work. End.

15
D G
Start. Work,– work,– work,– of art.
start as works of... ... To live our lives as works of art.
Start. Work. Work, work, work of art.

28. You Go Ahead

(from "Little Machines")

Secretary Michael

Like a Locomotive

♪ = 84

Upper

Middle

Lower

Got - ta get there, got - ta. Got - ta get there, got - ta. Got - ta get there, got - ta. Got - ta get there, got - ta.

Get there, got - ta get there. Get there, got - ta get there. Get there, got - ta get there. Get there, got - ta get there.

Got - ta get there, got - ta. Got - ta get there, got - ta. Got - ta get there, got - ta. Got - ta get there, got - ta.

B♭ E♭

You go a - head, I'm not in line.

(Train Whistle)

Get there, got - ta get there. Get there, got - ta get there. GET THERE! GET THERE!

Got - ta get there, got - ta. Got - ta get there, got - ta. Got - ta get there, got - ta. Got - ta get there, got - ta.

7
Bb
Eb
You go a - head,
I will be fine.
I'm
(Train Whistle)
Get there, got - ta get there. Get there, got - ta get there.
GET THERE!
GET THERE!
Got - ta get there, got - ta. Got - ta get there, got - ta.
Got - ta get there, got - ta. Got - ta get there, got - ta.
9
Bb
Eb
Bb
Eb
free
I'm
Get there, got - ta get there. Get there, got - ta get there.
Get there, got - ta get there. Get there, got - ta get there.
Got - ta get there, got - ta. Got - ta get there, got - ta.
Got - ta get there, got - ta. Got - ta get there, got - ta.
11
Bb
Eb
Bb
Eb
Free
to
(I'm)
free.
Get there, got - ta get there. Get there, got - ta get there. Get there, got - ta get there. Get there, got - ta get there.
free.
Got - ta get there, got - ta. Got - ta get there, got - ta. Got - ta get there, got - ta. Got - ta get there got - ta.
free.

Notes

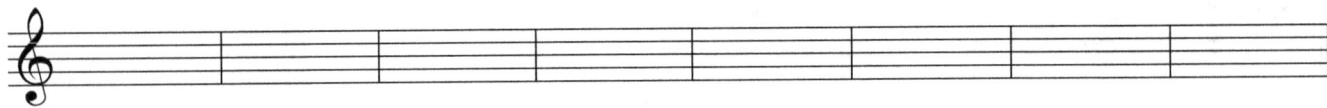

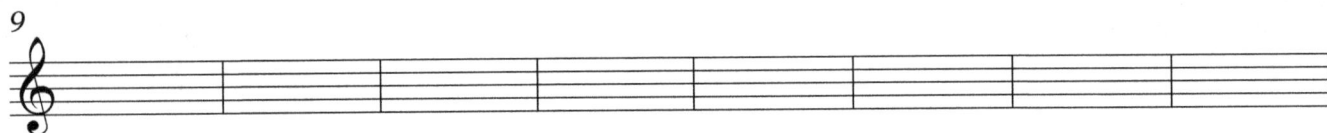

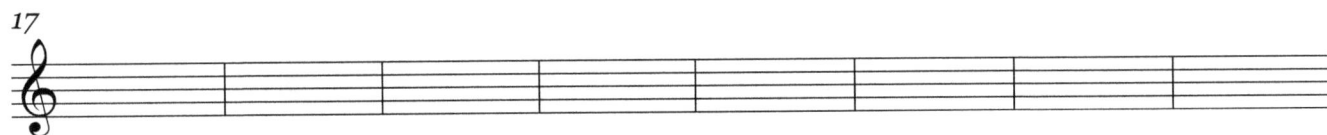

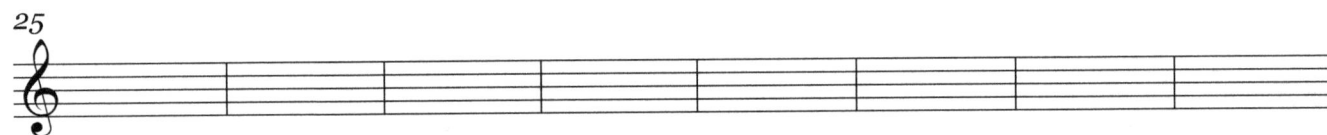

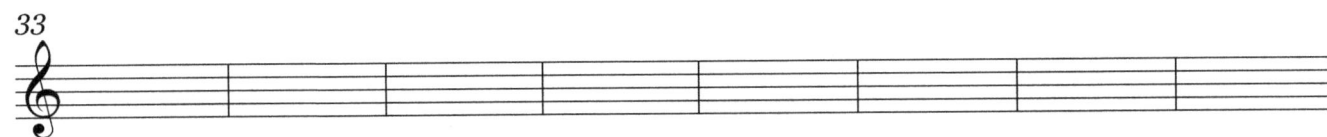

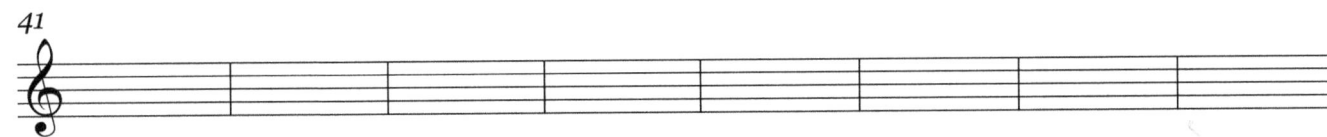

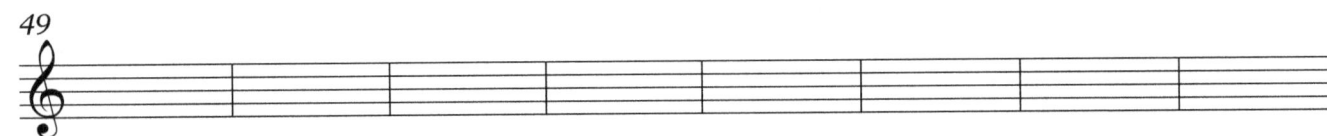

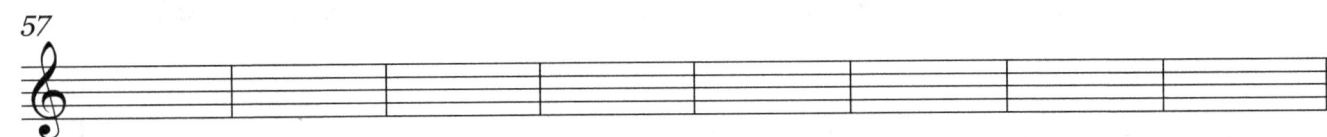

Recent Works by Secretary Michael

Jo Puma - Wild Choir Music
Collection of 36 traditional "Sacred Harp" arrangements with new secular lyrics for our diverse society. This collection has removed the 3 barriers that have kept this music out of our schools: inappropriate lyrics, poor shape-note legibility, and nonstandard use of standard solfege names. Now we all have a chance to experience this exciting early American music. (Book and free downloads available at "secretarymichael.com")

Secular Hymnal
Collection of 144 favorite hymn tunes from around the world. The hymn tunes have been re-notated and given thoughtful egalitarian lyrics that promote peace. Many public schools use them for choral sight-reading practice. Available in both unison/guitar and SATB choir editions. Now we all have a chance to share in these musical treasures. (Books and free downloads available at "secretarymichael.com")

Candelescence
A peace-themed opera/musical for singing groups of all ages. The story is about a young woman named "Twimfina" (an acronym for "The World Is My Family, I'm Not Afraid") who runs off to a hostile country. It is scored for voice and piano. Although rather long, the work is divided into 23 segments, many of which can stand alone. Many egalitarian songs. (Book and free downloads available at "secretarymichael.com")

Choral Dialectics
A "choral dialectic" is a 4-movement choral work (with or without instruments) in which a rational argument is battled-out musically. There's only one rule: every choral dialectic must use the following four titles for its four movements: "Principle" - "Argument" - "Counterargument" - "Resolution". The four choral dialectics by Secretary Michael are rousing to hear and fun to sing. (Books and free downloads available at "secretarymichael.com")

Aren't We the Lucky Ones
A book-length story about a group of college science students who share an understanding that there is no free will. They understand that there are no "good people" or "bad people", just lucky ones and unlucky ones. With this understanding comes the responsibility to protect the "unlucky" from the wrath of the "lucky". The students form a community in order to live out their ideals. (Book available - both paperback and digital)

Little Machines
A collection of 28 very short mechanical works for unaccompanied mixed singers. Full of ostinati and countermelodies, these well-crafted, sophisticated songs are easy and fun to sing - and fascinating to hear. (Book and free downloads available at "secretarymichael.com")

"Someday there will be groups of enlightened people who get together to sing choral music just for the simple joy of doing it. They won't be there to rehearse for some big concert. They won't be there to get academic credit or financial reward. They won't be there to wear choir robes and praise their god. They won't be there to march and salute their country. They'll just be there for the visceral and intellectual thrill of singing with other people. My purpose is to provide these 'Someday Choirs' with a body of free and open music worthy of their great adventure together."

- Secretary Michael

www.ingramcontent.com/pod-product-compliance
Lightning Source LLC
Chambersburg PA
CBHW081642040426
42449CB00015B/3429